WARWICKSHIRE DIALECT

SHAKESPEARE COUNTRY

A selection of words and anecdotes
from around Warwickshire

by
Brendan Hawthorne

BRADWELL
BOOKS

Published by Bradwell Books
9 Orgreave Close Sheffield S13 9NP
Email: books@bradwellbooks.co.uk

British Library Cataloguing in Publication Data:
a catalogue record for this book is available from the
British Library.

1st Edition

ISBN: 9781909914698

Print: Gomer Press, Llandysul, Ceredigion SA44 4JL

Artwork and design by: Andrew Caffrey

Photograph Credits: Shutterstock and Warwickshire
County Council Archives
(individual images credited WCCA).

Introduction

Welcome to Warwickshire!

Before we start I want you to imagine what it would be like listening back through centuries of speech patterns, and then try to tease out and recognise those roots in the way people from Warwickshire speak today, whether those word roots be Scandinavian, Northern European, Central European, Southern European – and, of course, whether they be Shakespearean!

Warwickshire was a meeting point not only for invading forces and settlers but also for industry and agriculture. If we travel from the industrialised north of the county to the more rural and agricultural south most visitors and locals alike will hear what is generally termed as a 'Midland' accent. Listen more closely and you will hear subtle shifts, from Coventry dialects through to 'light Brummy' and on to dialects more akin to the borders of Oxfordshire.

A thousand years ago the county of Warwickshire was seen administratively as part of the ancient Kingdom of Mercia. However, over the intervening years, Warwickshire's borders have changed considerably, gaining towns and villages with one stroke of the pen whilst others have been lost in shaping and defining the county as it is today.

I hope that you enjoy your journey through the pages of this book. Regard it as a taster, an invitation if you will, to look deeper into the stories, language and traditions of this ancient shire. This book has been written out of an intense interest in a beautiful county once described *'as typical a county as can be found anywhere'*, with both respect and humour!

Sculpture of the 'Bard' himself, William Shakespeare
Shutterstock/T.Fabian

11-22

Words

The following words have either a local (L) or Shakespearean (S) root in Warwickshire. Unmarked words are broader in origin or derivative of middle English. This is only a small taster of many possible inclusions. Your exploration of Warwickshire-related words and phrases starts here! For fun have a go at developing your own sentences when you become familiar with the words!

A

Abate – To shorten or to make blunt (S)

Abed – In bed, asleep (S)

Abhor – To show horror, recoil or disdain (S)

Aboveabit – Extremely, the best (L)

Abridgement – A short play (S)

Acomen – Coming, as in coming along (L)

Addiction – A tendency towards, prone to (S)

Affy – To trust (S)

Afore – Before, firstly (S)

Agood – A large amount (S)

A-night – At night (S)

Animil – Animal (L)

Anklebiter – Young child, toddler (L)

Antick – An old fashioned fool (S)

Apricock – Apricot (S)

A-thatten – Like that, that one

Athissen – Like this, this one

Avaunt – Go away (S)

Averring – Confirming

B

Bab – A term of endearment for female (or youngest female) (L)

Babbies – Babies (L)

Baccarre – Held or kept back (S)

Badder – Worse (L)

Baddest – Worst (L)

Balk – To hesitate (S)

Ballett – A song, a ballad of rhyming couplets (L)

Barm – Yeasty froth on fermenting ale (S)

Batch – Small round loaf or cob (L)

Bate – To flutter as in the wings of a hawk – Lose or diminish (S)

Batlet – A tool for laundering clothes (L)

Bavin – A useless leftover, firewood, kindling (S)

Bayent – Am not, as in I am not doing that

Bedazzle – Blinded by light, brilliance or science! (S)

Bedduth – Bedworth, the town of… (L)

Beeyers – Beers (L)

Belt – Hit hard (L)

Berattle – Abuse, go on endlessly (S)

Beshrew – Befall evil (S)

Bess – Bus (L)

Beteem – Let out, allow, give, grant (S)

Biffer – An unattractive person (L)

Billitt – Stick of firewood or kindling (L)

Birmenghum/Brummagem – Birmingham (L)

Blab – A gossip, someone who spreads rumours (L)

Blarting – Crying out loud, hysteria (L)

Blench – A quick look, at a glance (S)

Blent – Blended (S)

Bloodboltered – Covered in blood (S)

Blowze – A woman or wench, usually a flushed or red-faced lady (S)

Bodkin – A dagger (S)

Bokenade – Egg or milk thickened stew

Bombast – Padding, overblown (S)

Bosky – Wooded, full of thorny thickets (S)

Bost – Burst, break open

Bote – Bought (L)

Bots – Maggots (L)

Brave – Handsome, bold, daring (S)

Broach – Start, draw out, pierce (S)

Broche – Spit roast

C

Cade – A small barrel or cask sometimes contains a quantity of fish (S)

Caggie-handed – Left handed

Cain-coloured – Redhead (L)

Caitiff – A prisoner (S)

Canstick – Candlestick (S)

Chaps – Cracks or small gaps

Chargeours – Large dishes or dished plates

Chawf – Warm

Chiken – Headland (L)

Chops – Thrusts, a violent shove (L) or mouth (S)

Chuck or **Shuck** – A term of endearment (L)

Chuck – Throw, chuck a ball (L)

Chuddy – Chewing gum (L)

Coil – Distress, trouble (S)

Cony-catch – To cheat, trap (S)

Cop - Catch – when giving or handing something to someone – *cop that* (L)

Copped off/pulled – Chatted up someone and succeeded in a 'romantic' rendezvous! (L)

Corsey, the – Pavement (L)

Cot-quean – Man who works as housewife. Meddler in domestic affairs (S)

Cote – Cottage (S)

Countervail – Outweigh, countervail one situation over another (S)

Cozier – Cobbler (S)

Crank – A winding passage way (S)

Cullion – A low-life, a man lacking morality (S)

Curby – Game of gutters (L)

Cut, the – Canal (L)

D

Daint – Did not; 'I daint do that' (L)

Deal fence – Dividing boundary or fence (L)

Dearn – Lonely (S)

Deboshed – Drunken, debauched (S)

De Di (Dee Dye) – A local ice cream manufacturer (Foleshill): *to have a De Di*

Diet – A piece of land (L) Way of life (S)

Doddell – A tree or similar with branches cut down, pollard (L)

Dole – A meadow shared between different tenants or owners (L)

Dolly – Used to wash laundry. Long wooden handle with four pegs – attached to a disc base. Used for agitating clothing when washing them (L)

Don – To put on

Donnies – Hands (sometimes dannies) (L)

Doofah – General term for an item when the correct

word doesn't come to mind!

Also used for a 'rude' part of the anatomy (L)

Drab – A lady of ill repute (L)

Draw – To bring near, call to

Droive – Drive (L)

Drownded – Drowned (L)

Druv – To drive as in drive a car

Dussn't – Dare not, wouldn't (L)

E

Egal – Equal, (egalitarian)

Eira one – Either (L)

Eld – Old, previous generations (S)

Emboss – Stalk or follow with evil/mortal intent (S)

Englut – Eat greedily (S)

Entry – Path or passageway between two terraced houses (L)

Ert – It (L)

Ett – Ate (L)

Evera – Every (L)

Expedience – Quickness, speed (S)

F

Fadge – To suit (S)

Fain – Gladly (S)

Fallow – Fawn in colour, unsown land or field (S)

Fancy – To desire (S)

Fap – Drunk (S)

Farst – Fast, as in quickly (L)

Fear – To scare or frighten

Feodary – A steward, in the stewardship of under the feudal system

Feodary – An accomplice (S)

Fettle – Prepare or make ready (L)

Firk – Reprimand, scold (S)

Fleer – Sneer at (L)

Foive – Five (L)

Forswear – Break word or promise (S)

Fosset – A small pipe to carry liquid, from the brewery trade (L)

Fote – Fought, I fote and lost (L)

Frit – Frightened, scared off (L)

Front – To oppose, show effrontery, object to

Fub off – To delay, cheat or rob (S)

Fustering – Mouldy (S)

Fustian – Pompous (S)

G

Gad – In haste, spur of moment, gad off – rush away (L)

Gage – Challenge, test (S)

Gallow – To scare (S)

Gast – Scared, aghast (S)

Grave – Serious, to inter

Gid – Gave (L)

Giz – Gives (L)

Gleek – A 16th-century card game or to taunt (S)

Gob – Mouth – from the name given to the mouth of a pit (L)

Goo – Goes (L)

Gobbies – Large marbles like gobstoppers (L)

Godcake – A triangular pastry or a small triangular reservation where three roads meet (L)

Gore – Lowest piece of land, a dip in contour (L)

Grize – A step

Grun – Grind (L)

Guinea – A value of currency. It was a pound and a shilling. £1.05 today

H

Hacked off – Fed up (L)

Hade – Headland (L)

Heavy – Sad or painful

Hern – Hers: 'I gave hern to him' (L)

Hie – A shrine

Honest – Pure

Honey-stalks – Clover (S)

Hook – A projected spit of land

I

I-grounde – Mince as in mincemeat
Inch meal – Bit by bit (L)
Inherit – Given or belief, possess (S)
Intpinse – Mess, confusion, tangle (S)

J

Jack – A mean person (S)
Jackert – Jacket (sometimes jack e') (L)
Jack-the-lad – A spirited youth –
Jetty/Jitty – Short cut between houses, usually between the back gardens, of two parallel streets (L)
Judicious – Fair, balanced or critical (S)

K

Kayed – Hand-reared as in kayed chicken (L)
Kep – Keep (L)
Kid – Bundle of items (L)
Knap – To hit or give a glancing blow (S)
Knave – A young boy, servant (S)

L

Lamp – To hit or punch (L)

Land – Yard

Lapsed – Overcome with shock or surprise, taken (S)

Lav, the – Toilet (L)

Lockram – Coarse linen (S)

Loony tick – Lunatic (L)

Lowt – Contempt or a clown (S)

Lozal – Someone who is a extravagant and wasteful (S)

Luce – Pike – river fish (S)

Lynch – Riverside access (L)

M

Mad – Wild or crazy

Maiden or peggy tub – A deep container or barrel shaped vessel for washing clothes in

Malkin – Servant (female) (S)

Mallecho – Mischief (S)

Mammock – To break or tear (S)

Mardy – Irritable (L)

Marlies – Marbles (L)

Massuve – Massive (L)

Mate – Match as in partner

Maunt – May not (L)

Mawkin – A dirty person, someone with poor personal hygiene (L)

Me bab – Term of endearment (L)

Med – Made, I med this for you (L)

Me duck – Term of endearment (L)

Mell – To mix or meddle (S)

Mickel/Mickle – Great or much (S)

Misery guts – Moody person (L)

Mizzling – Light rain or drizzle (L)

Moonish – Changeable, dreamy and unfocused (L)

Mow – To pull a face or grimace (L)

Murch – Much (L)

Mure – A wall (S)

N

Nayword – A buzz word or a move towards denial (S)

Neeld – A needle (L)

Neif – Hand (S)

Ninny – A fool or nincompoop (S)

Nobbies – Crusts of bread (L)

Nodder – Condom (L)

Note – List

Now just – A short while back (L)

Nowl – Head (S)

Half timbered buildings in Warwick
Shutterstock/Tupungato

O

Oadhouse – Wode house, a place for dying (L)

O'erwrowt – Overcome (S)

Oice Skayen – Ice skating (L)

Oidea – Idea (L)

Oojamacallit – Thingybob or thingammybob; indefinite description of forgotten word for item (L)

On ett – Of it (L)

Ought – Privy to or promised to (L)

16

Ourgate – A holiday destination for those who couldn't afford one! Play on words, based on e.g. Margate, Ramsgate etc.

Ourn – Ours (L)

Ousel-cock – Blackbird (L)

Ovown – Of our own (L)

P

Painful – Difficult

Pall – To wrap up (S)

Palmy – Victorious, with success (S)

Parrock – A land enclosure (L)

Particoat – To cover in colourful fabric or garb (clothes) (S)

Pash – To strike or hit (L)

Peggy tub – Laundry bucket or tub (L)

Perpend – To think of

Pept – Peeped (L)

Persun – Person (L)

Pew-fellow – A friend or colleague (S)

Piece – Sandwich (L)

Pike – An irregular, pointed piece of land at the side of a field

Pikelets – Crumpets (L)

Pinfold – A confine for lost cattle (S)

Pingle – Long narrow strip of land or field (L)

Pipkin – A covered earthenware cooking vessel

Pippin – Apple or colloquial term for female breast

Planched – Boarded

Pleck – A small enclosed piece of land also hemplock and pightie (L)

Poor John – Herring (L)

Porrege – Porridge (L)

Posher/posser – Used to wash laundry. A wooden handle with a plunger shaped attachment in wood, copper or zinc. Used to 'punch' – clothes when washing them in a maiden tub (L)

Potch – To push with violence (S)

Practerse – Practise (L)

Prank – To dress up

Prate – Chatter without purpose

Prick-song – Song that is sung in parts

Pugging – Thieving (S)

Pumps – Plimsols, soft sports shoe (L)

Puttock – A kite (S)

Q

Quaint – Beautiful, fancy or ornate

Quake – To shake or tremble with fear

Quat – Pimple or spot (L)

Quicklay – Quickly (L)

Quillet – A small close or cul-de-sac

R

Raddock/ruddock – Robin (L)

Rapture – An ecstatic fit (S)

Rase – Tuberous root as in ginger (L)

Rat-Tat-Tat-Ginger – A game of knocking doors and running away before the door is answered (L)

Ratted – Drunk (L)

Ravin – A destructive hunger or desire (S)

Reechy – Dirty, filthy (L/S)

Respect – Consideration

Retire – To go to bed, to retreat to rest (S)

Rheumy – Moist (mainly to do with eyes and mouth)

Rigol – A circle (S)

Rive – Split open

Ronvon – Contemptuous word referring to a woman (S)

Rouse – A measure of spirit (L)

Rummel – A mess or rubbish. An old term for a soak-away or a pit of rubble.

S

Sallies – Advancements especially in battle

Scantling – A small portion (S)

Screase – Taking a breather, to rest between exertions

Scrumpen – Scrumping, as in apples (L)

Selfsame – Of its own type

Sentermental – Sentimental (L)

Shees'n – Hers (L)

Shewned – To show

Shoon – Shoes

Shore – Support or buttress

Shrift – To admit, confession

Shrive – To confess

Simmer down – Calm down (L)

Simular – False, forgery

Sin – See (L)

Singen – Singing (L)

Sippet – Toasted bread

Sith/Sithence – Since

Slang – A long and narrow piece of ground (L)

Slug-abed – Lazy person (L)

Smidge/smidgen – A small amount (L)

Snap – Food (L)

Sneeped/sneaped – Offended, taunted, snubbed or cut off

Snuff – To take offence

Soide – Side (L)

Sot – Sat/sit (L)

Sot – A fool (S)

Spang – A salient point of land (L)

Sperr – To bolt, fasten or enclose (S)

Spial – Spy

Spilth – Spilling

Spitting – Wind-blown light rain (L)

Sprog – Offspring, child (L)

Squiny – Narrow eyed, squint (L)

Steff – Stuff (L)

Still – Lasting

Strote – Strode or strutted (L)

Struv – Strive (L)

Subscription – To follow or show obedience to

Suff – Drain (L)

Swep – Sweep (L)

Swinge-buckler – A bully (S)

T

Take – To take over or overcome

Tat-tars – To go out (L)

Tax – Blame or criticise (S)

Teggies – Teeth (L)

Territry – Territory (L)

Testy – Troubling, as in a troubling time (S)

Thee – You, as in thee can say what thee thinks

Thine – Yours, as in 'this is thine'

This'n – This way (L)

Thou – You, as in 'thou art a beauty'

Thine – Yours

Thrid – Thread (L)

Thy – Your, as in 'thy book is much overdue'

Toimes – Times (L)

Tootsies – Feet (L)

Treacle Town – Nuneaton, known for jam making (L)

Trigon – Triangle (S)

Tuck – Sweets, or more general term for a light snack (L)

Tundish – Funnel

Tyer – Tire (L)

U

Unbarbed – Untrimmed or without armour (S)

Unclew – Undo, ruin

Urchin – Hedgehog (L)

Undergo – To take on

Unpregnant – Lacking thought or substance, inane (S)

V

Vail – Lower, sinking (S)

Vaunt – Boast, excessive praise

Vile – Evil (anag.) Hateful, disgusting

Villerge – Village (L)

Vindicative – Vengeful, retaliatory (S)

Vizament – Advertisement, consultation

W

Wall-eyed – Shocked, with wide eyes (S)

Wampy – Mad, insane (L)

Want – in need of, lacking

Warrener – Gamekeeper (S)

Waygoose – An annual employer's outing (L)

Whadya reckon? – What do you think? (L)

Whipcord – A knotted piece of cord worn by men to indicate that they were looking for work (L)

Writhled – Shrivelled up

Y

Yare – Quick to respond, nimble (S)

Yerk – To lash out quickly and without warning (S)

Yest – Foam or froth – yesty (S)

Young – Recent (S)

Z

Zany – Crazy buffoonery (S)

Zew – Zoo (L)

Ex-LNER B12 steam locomotive 8572 at Toddington with a head of
steam on the Gloucestershire Warwickshire Railway Shutterstock/i4lcocl2

Over the years and through the centuries, rivers, canals,
railways and roads have all brought and served their own
brands of industry, commerce and leisure to Warwickshire.
They have connected the coal and manufacturing industries
of the north of the region with the rest of the country. They
have allowed agriculture to trade further afield, as well as
drawing great numbers of visitors to the county to see its
many splendours from towns, villages and countryside to
the *bardic* literature of Stratford.

Now for something to get your teggies into!

Some sayings from North Warks

THREE SPIRES – COVENTRY

'*Sending someone to Coventry*' is a term believed to date back to the Civil War. St John's Church in Coventry was a Parliamentarian stronghold and it was where Royalist soldiers were held. They were obviously given a cool reception there! Being '*sent to Coventry*' is now taken to mean a conspiracy of silence towards an individual.

A 'half-whipped' or half timbered Warwickshire barn
Shutterstock/Andrew Roland

You've got a mouth from here to Broadgate! –
A loudmouth or gossip

Question: Where are you going?
Answer: Up Nick's the back of the Rudge!
Meaning: I'm going out and mind your own business!
The Rudge was a local factory.

Over the bridge – Bedworth and Nuneaton from a Coventry perspective.

A Brummagem screwdriver – A Birmingham screwdriver is a local 'metal bashing' term for a hammer!

Up the wooden hill to Sheet Lane to play shut eye in the field – Going to bed.

Go down the town for shopping – (Coventry)

Go up the City for football – (Coventry)

The old five – An old term used to describe Coventry City Football Club

'Shot from the top of Tuttle Hill' (Nuneaton) or **'Thrown in from the Broadgate'** (Coventry) – A pie with not much filling becomes a general term for something lacking substance.

'As true as Coventry blue' means the real thing, trustworthy, genuine, lasting. Coventry blue was a dye used in the medieval period and was known not to fade.

Coventry speak also puts the word 'the' in front of place names and the such like! An example of this would be: going down to *the* Broadgate.

Shakespeare's birthplace taken from the Trousset Encyclopaedia
1886 -1891 Shutterstock/Morphart Creation

A few quotes from the Bard himself

'For such as we are made of, such we be.
How will this fadge? My master loves her dearly;'
FROM TWELFTH NIGHT

'O thou pernicious caitiff! How came you, Cassio, by that
handkerchief. That was my wife's?'
FROM OTHELLO

'But beshrew my jealousy! By heaven, it is as proper to our age.'
FROM HAMLET

'Avaunt, you cullions!'
FROM HENRY V

'Men are April when they woo, December when they wed.
Maids are May when they are maids, but the sky changes when
they are wives.'
FROM AS YOU LIKE IT

'Hell is empty, all the devils are here.'
FROM THE TEMPEST

'As soon go kindle fire with snow, as seek to quench the
fire of love with words'
FROM TWO GENTLEMEN OF VERONA

Royal Shakespeare Theatre, Stratford-upon-Avon
Shutterstock/Gail Johnson

Some fun with conversational Shakespeare!

I commend thee! Thou art indeed in rude health.

Hello! You look well.

Good sir! Attend thee here! Thou can see anon that we are desirous of libation. Come apace and let us be drawn on your finest bastarde!

Barman! You can see we are in need of getting drunk.

Be quick and pour us some of your best Spanish wine!

Thou art base yet fortune has favoured thee. And of this bold enterprise it has brought thee great riches.

You don't deserve it but you've done all right for yourself.

SHAKESPEARE had quite a few words and phrases in his works relating to falconry as not only was it a popular sport but it also gave the opportunity to the author to add drama to chasing or tracking down a situation within a play. Here are a few terms that relate to falconry which have now been accepted in broader language usage, arguably as a result of inclusion in the many works of Shakespeare.

Fed Up

When a hawk's 'crop is full', meaning it has gorged to its fill on prey, it will not want to hunt but only rest and digest. This term was taken to mean a person was fed up when they had had their fill of a particular situation.

Hoodwinked or Falcon in Hood

A leather hood is used in falconry training to keep the bird calm by closing down its extremely sensitive vision to avoid excitable distractions. Without the hood the bird would see many things to interest it that the handler wouldn't and this would therefore stress the bird. To force the bird to concentrate on the chosen target he 'hoodwinks' the bird. This meaning now refers to someone who has been duped. Commonly used when someone feels that they have been tricked into something. They could then be termed as hoodwinked into something they didn't want to do.

Chaperon

Derives from an old French word also meaning hood, in particular, a hood for a bird of prey. The French took this word to mean protector and in English the root of the word was used and became 'chaperone' to mean a caring companion.

Callow

Callow refers in the main to infancy or youth. It means someone or something that is inexperienced and forms the expression 'callow youth'; rarely is it associated with old age. The word originally meant 'bare' or 'bald' – but in falconry it describes a young bird moulting its downy feathers.

Booze

Depending on who you ask, a 'house' or 'bows' is either a raptor's drinking bowl or describes the way a bird drinks. Apparently, given the chance, raptors tend to eat or drink to excess (and thus become 'fed up'). Obviously, humans would never do anything like that, but nevertheless 'house' has been re-spelt over the years to 'booze' and has taken the meaning of drinking too much (particularly alcohol) and has also been 'nouned' to become a generic term for alcoholic drinks.

Codger

This word is always used when relating to someone or something with experience! Within falconry terms a falcon's perch was traditionally known as a 'cadge'. When a falconer eventually became too old for hunting and hung up the gauntlets as it were, they would be given the job of carrying the cadge into the field. This would have given rise to the term 'cadger' and eventually 'old cadger'. Through time this would change to the familiar and friendly respectful term we use today of someone being an old codger! Being 'on the cadge' can often refer to someone on the take and expecting things for nothing.

Haggard

A haggard is a falcon that is caught in the wild as a fully grown adult, in the main around the end of their migration when they were weak, thin and bedraggled. The term is now used to mean someone who looks thin and tired. The word 'hag' also comes from this root, meaning an old, wrinkled and feeble-looking woman.

Gorge

This is a term used to describe overeating, 'gorge' being another word for throat. This is where the term for a deep valley comes from. A bird's throat is also called a gorge and the throat feathers are called the gorget, which also gives name to the piece of armour that protects the throat. Birds often store food in their mouths and this is where gorging your food started to apply to us humans!

Rouse

This is yet another old French word that this time describes hawks shaking their feathers. We often use the term 'shake your feathers' to encourage someone to wake up or we see them rouselling up!

Under his thumb or wrapped around his/her little finger

A falcon is tethered by a leash called a jess to stop it from making its own way in life. When the bird is on the falconer's arm the falconer will put part of the jess 'under his thumb' or 'wrap it around his little finger' to keep the bird under control. So in today's parlance to be under the thumb or wrapped around someone's little finger means we are under the control of another.

With bated breath

The term 'bated' usually only ever appears as part of a phrase: 'with bated breath we await the dawn', meaning we hold our breath until dawn. It first appears in The Merchant of Venice:

Shall I bend low and in a bondman's key,
With bated breath and whispering humbleness, Say this:

'Fair sir, you spit on me on Wednesday last;
You spurn'd me such a day; another time
You call'd me dog; and for these courtesies
I'll lend you thus much moneys'?

When a hawk is tethered it is referred to as 'bated', meaning the bird is restrained, a shortened form of the word 'abated' which means 'restrained.'

Caesar's Tower, Kenilworth Castle
Shutterstock/Morphart Creation

Warwickshire Foundations

Much of 21st-century Warwickshire could be regarded as a leafy shire with major towns and cities that have grown up within what could be regarded as a traditional English countryside setting. It is unlike its near neighbour, Birmingham, and even more so the post-industrial landscapes of the Black Country. But if we dig below the surface of the Warwickshire soil we find far more 'industry' than can be perceived today.

Small-scale quarries bloomed as settlements became villages, and building materials and road metal were needed for medieval period infrastructure. Wood came from the Forest of Arden and gave the recognisable look of the half-timbered/timber-framed properties which can still be seen today.

Various sandstones and coloured limestones were readily available for building materials that defined the type and colour of the building within an area, and most villages had their own small-scale quarries to accommodate local demand. This in turn provided work for quarrymen to dig and masons to dress. Warwickshire also sits on clay and, therefore, provided the base material for brick manufacture. Then, of course, you need something to bind these blocks together. In the south of the region cement and lime manufacture took place. Many local industries didn't survive or were no longer viable once the Industrial Revolution took place and heavy material became easier to transport via canals, roads and railways. Warwickshire became more of an 'importer' of such goods from its near neighbours to the west. Remnants of this cottage industry past can still be seen in place names, street names and public house names. Have a look and spot the echoes of Warwickshire's past for yourself.

The old blacksmith shop, Preston-on-Stour.
WCCA

North Warwickshire, however, did continue to produce industrial quantities of much-needed domestic and power station coal from a seam known to the Romans in the fourth century. The seam was mined up until the closures in the 1980s and runs from north-west of Atherstone to south of Nuneaton. At its peak at the end of the nineteenth century the mining industry boasted over thirty collieries producing Warwickshire coal.

Some beliefs and superstitions of the mineworkers

In most areas of the country there are a lot of general superstitions. One area of industry known for its culture of superstitions relates directly to mines and the safety of the miners themselves. A list of superstitions was common and is usually read as follows:

Don't you ever go to the pit if you've dreamt of a broken clog or if the fire in your house has gone out overnight as this foretells of danger.

If you meet a woman on the way to the pit turn around and go back home as it's a sure sign of death.

If you see bright lights in the mine turn and run as fast as you can from the pit.

If you hear a howling from the pit this is Gabriel's Hounds, so leave the pit and return on the next day.

If you should smell a sulphurous stale stench at the pit it is a sure sign that imps have been at play so go home for your own safety.

If you want to send the evil spirits from a pit, walk in with a bible in your right hand and say the Lord's Prayer. That will keep you safe and send them on their way!

Farming and associated industries

In Warwickshire it could be argued that farming has not only been the largest combined industry but also the most enduring. Over many centuries the land has been worked in this county that gave rise to associated and allied industries such as smithying, wheelwrights and cart builders. Then there were the refining industries and trades that developed over time, which included millers, bakers, brewers, pub landlords and shopkeepers.

Field work

Some areas of Warwickshire have been farmed for at least five thousand years. In East Warwickshire villages became a hub of three to four very large fields that were then divided down for individual tenants or freeholders to farm. If you look at the landscape even today you will still find evidence of 'ridge and furrow' lines.

Pea pickers at Broom circa 1910
WCCA

There is a general rule for gauging how old a field may be. If you have time and it is safe to do so pace a hundred steps along a hedgerow and count the number of different trees or shrubs within that particular section. A hedgerow is said to gain one new species of tree per hundred years. Find five different species and you have a five-hundred-year-old hedgerow!

The Forest of Arden in West Warwickshire had areas of its trees cleared into odd-shaped little fields for local farming. Many names were given to these smallholdings including, spang, pleck, hemplock and pingle. This sort of land management kept farms small, unlike strip farming where one strip could be added to another and a hard-working peasant could be become a rich person.

Some farming superstitions

When relying on a successful harvest merely to survive, much care and land husbandry came through anecdotal plant lore and written almanacs. This, in turn, gave rise to superstitions relating to successful harvests and an avoidance of ruin both financial and nutritional. The following is taken from records which placed witchcraft at the top of the list for any type of failure, including death of horses or cattle, stoppage of milk production, beer not fermenting or butter not setting.

In 1875 a labourer was convinced that an elderly lady was to blame for misfortune at Long Compton. He took it upon himself 'to rid her of life' as he felt he was under her spell. In his defence he said that she was 'the properest witch I ever knowed!'

Workers Union Fete – Prize winners 1924, Southan
WCCA

Other related superstitions

Mad as a hatter?

The following describes the term 'as mad as a hatter.' This illness was caused by prolonged exposure to mercury and its vapour, which was commonly used in the manufacture of felt and in colouring and stabilising the material up until the twentieth century.

The man affected is easily upset and embarrassed, loses all joy in life and lives in constant fear of being dismissed from his job. He has a sense of timidity and may lose self-control before visitors. Thus, if

41

Pickering hat makers
WCCA

one stops to watch such a man in a factory, he will sometimes throw down his tools and turn in anger on the intruder, saying he cannot work if watched. Occasionally a man is obliged to give up work because he can no longer take orders without losing his temper or, if he is a foreman, because he has no patience with men under him. Drowsiness, depression, loss of memory and insomnia may occur, but hallucinations, delusions and mania are rare. The most characteristic symptom, though it is seldom the first to appear, is mercurial tremor. It is neither as fine nor as regular as that of hyperthyroidism. It may be interrupted every few minutes by coarse jerky movements. It usually begins in the fingers, but the eyelids, lips and tongue are affected early. As it progresses it passes to the arms and legs, so that it becomes very difficult for a man to walk about the workshop, and he may have to be guided to his bench. At this stage the condition is so obvious that it is known to the layman as 'hatter's shakes.'

(BUCKELL ET AL., *Chronic Mercury Poisoning, 1946*)

Needle making

In the eighteenth century cottage industries (working from home) were common and employed many people on a local level. Their goods were collected for market or transported by the families themselves to find buyers for their product. The people of Redditch hand-made needles for the then newly forming textile industries where through the use of water power the wire was forged, drawn, pointed and polished at the needle mills along the rivers Alne and Arrow to the towns of Studley and Alcester.

Minerva needle works
WCCA

Other wares and oojimacallits

Birmingham was once in Warwickshire along with the manufacturing towns of Meriden and Coventry. Including what was deemed lighter manufacturing and the production of white metal goods from coins and jewellery in Birmingham to sewing machines, bikes, cars and kitchen wares and equipment in other areas of the county, it can be seen that Warwickshire is a very diverse county whose history has been rich in change and development to suit the needs of its settlers and neighbours.

Kenilworth was known for its lantern widows, cutlery handles, mugs, spoons and books made from animal horn. Leather was also tanned here and at Nuneaton for general use in saddlery, clothing, shoes and book binding. Up until the middle of the twentieth century the region had over thirty manufacturers of hats in the north of the county. To make hats you need the fur of small animals such as rabbits, as well as water and wool, and these were all in plentiful supply. Water power drove the mills and machinery before steam and electricity took over respectively. Around the Coventry area silk winding and ribbon weaving were major local employers through the late eighteenth century and into the early nineteenth centuries that led to larger and more general textile industries in more modern times.

Lady with motorcycle in the 1920s
WCCA

Recipes from across the region and through time

Now, most people like to get their gastric juices flowing over a favourite meal, and as some of these recipes go back over many centuries they have certainly stood up to the rigours of time, taste and fashion! Just think, you could be soon serving up a meal that fuelled the writing talents of Mr Shakespeare himself. Who knows what play evolved from the after effects of one of these wonderful recipes!

VYAUND DE CYPRYS BASTARDE

(All right, there's no need to be like that about it!)

This recipe dates back to the medieval period and will easily fill a hollow stomach before going up the wooden hill to sheet lane, especially if you've got a nice, freshly baked batch that's just sitting waiting for the right accompaniment to come along! Now, before we go off on the wrong tack, *Bastarde* is a term used for spiced honey-sweetened Spanish wine.

So what do you need to get on and start this intriguing dish?

The main bit is made from 800g of minced chicken with 300ml of chicken stock and the same in Spanish red wine. You then need to have to hand a tablespoon of honey with half a teaspoon of each of ground mace, ginger, galangal, cinnamon, cloves and allspice and black pepper. A handful of fresh parsley and two tablespoons of rice flour should be kept in readiness and you'll also need to steep a pinch of saffron stems in warm water as well as beat four egg yolks.

And so we begin!

Boileth the i-grounde chicken most fowl (sic) in the stock and simmereth for ten minutes. Whilst the fowl cooks choppeth the parsley finely! Skimmeth impurities from the broiling broth to leave a clear rue and then addeth all herbe, honey and spice except saffron. Stir all ingredients and reduce by a quarter of its volume. When the saffron has coloured the water and softened add to the mix. In a small cup stir the rice flour with two tablespoons of broth liquid and add with the egg yolks to the broth, stirring all the time. Bring to the boil and stir until it thickens. If the recipe is too sweet add salt. Too sour; add honey.

Now to the best part!

Serveth in a bowl and dip your batch!

BEEF STEW BESTOWED UPON SIPPETS

In the early part of the 17th century a man by the name of Sir Kenelm Digby, a Buckinghamshire lad who travelled a lot, decided to publish notes on his likes and here is one of them! This is a good wholesome stew and would drive the cold out on any chilly day. First of all though, dear reader, you may ask what a sippet is? Well, you could turn back to the dictionary or I could tell you that it is simply slices of toasted bread! And before we go any further a pipkin is a covered earthenware pot like a tagine and is of French design. A casserole dish will do fine if you don't have a crock pot.

So tenderize and cube a kilogram of beef and roll in four tablespoons of seasoned plain flour. Fry the beef in four tablespoons of butter, adding two large sliced onions as you go. When all is cooked and brown place the beef and onions in the bottom of your cooking pot, adding half a litre of good red wine and the same in beef stock. Add an anchovy with salt and pepper to taste and the following: chopped parsley and tyme (a tablespoon of each), a bayleaf and half a teaspoon i-grounde of each of the following: allspice, ginger, cinnamon and nutmeg. Stir and bring to the boil for a few minutes and then cover and slow cook for two hours either on top of the hob or in the oven. Now while that's going on, get a small handful of marigold petals if you have them to hand and twenty minutes before cooking time add the petals and season further to taste removing the lid to thicken if needs be.

Serve upon sippets and add seasonal vegetables if required as a side serving. *I'm hungry just writing about it!*

COVENTRY GODCAKES

Go to the shoppes and get somme good puff pastry, which on your return you will need to roll out to a thicknesse of a gold sovereign. If you don't have the filling ingredients get those as well! Now with care, cut into pieces eight and a bit inches by seven inches approximately.

To make your fruit filling melt four ounces of butter and add half a pound of currants and a quarter of finely chopped mixed peel. Add a teaspoon of mixed spice and half a teaspoon of ground cinnamon as well as two ounces of sugar. Add rum or brandy to taste if so required!

Get a tablespoon of your cooled mincemeat (do not use bought mincemeat with suet in it as it won't cook in time) and place in the middle of each of your pastry pieces. Now fold diagonally or corner to corner across the parcel to make a triangle. Wet the edges where they meet and pinch together. Flatten the parcel slightly and slash the top along the length three times to let the steam vent forth. Brush with egg white and sprinkle with caster sugar and then bake in a hot oven until risen and golden brown.

COVENTRY GINGERBREAD

Again checketh most thoroughly that you have all of the ingredients before startinge! Take six ounces of brown flour and add three ounces of castor sugar and a teaspoon of ground ginger and stir the dry mixture thoroughly. Lightly rubbe in four ounces of butter and two ounces of chopped fresh ginger. When the mixture become crumbly place on a greased sandwich tinne and press lightly into position. Bake at gas mark three or 125 degrees for ten minutes. Break up when cool and indulge yourself!

WARWICKSHIRE SCONES

Take a goodly eight ounces of self-raising flour, sieve and add a quarter teaspoon of baking powder, also adding a quarter teaspoon of salt as you go.

Rub in two ounces of butter and add a tablespoon of honey mixed with three tablespoons of milk. Add milk (up to 150ml in total) until you get a soft but not sticky dough.

Turn out the dough onto a floured borde and knead lightly with your fingertips before rolling out to a three quarter inch thicke square. Cut into circles or triangles and brush with milk. Place on a floured oven tinne and bake in a hot oven (230°C) for about ten minutes. When the scones are cooked they should sound hollow if you tap them on their bottom. *Remember, they will be hot!*

Put the kettle on and make your favourite brew and serve your scones with honey or jam and butter or cream! Congratulate yourself on making your own regional cream tea!

A half-timbered cottage at Shottery
Shutterstock/David Hughes

Some Warwickshire traditions and festivals

The Atherstone Ball Game, 'The Match of Gold'

One Shrove Tuesday afternoon in the twelfth century during the reign of King John someone decided to have a game of football in the streets of Atherstone. This game has been played there ever since on this day with the specially made ball (heavy leather and decorated with red, white and blue ribbons; usually this large ball has contained three bladders!) being thrown out to the crowd by some local personality who usually chucks coins to the children assembled in payment for the ball.

Shop windows are boarded up before the game commences, and the match is usually played between Warwickshire and Leicestershire, boasts hundreds of players and lasts two gruelling hours! It can only be described as a 'free-for-all'! It is played along the old Roman Road of Watling Street. There are no goals and no rules apart from one: do not kill fellow players! The ball is thrown into the crowd from Barclays Bank at 3pm for the game to commence and after 4.30pm the ball can be hidden or deflated legally. The winner is the team of the player left holding the ball when time is called. The individual is allowed to keep the ball as a memento of the spectacle.

Lady Godiva

The legend of LADY GODIVA (*Lady Godgifu, 'God's gift' in Anglo-Saxon*) became more widely known in the thirteenth century, a good two hundred years after GODIVA's death. She was recorded as a widow when marrying KING LEOFRIC, Earl of Mercia. The couple became generous benefactors of religious establishments and founded a Benedictine monastery that was built on the ruins of a nunnery after the Danes had demolished it earlier. In short, the money had to come from somewhere and this was in the form of taxation. The people of Coventry were poor and were poorer still under the regime of heavy taxation. GODIVA took pity on the people and pleaded with her husband time and again to reduce the tax levies on his subjects, and in particular horse tax. One day he relented and agreed to reduce taxation if she would ride through the streets of Coventry naked and on horseback, her virtue being maintained only by her long tresses of hair. She agreed to this and appealed to the people of Coventry to shutter their windows and close their doors so as not to see her as she rode through the streets on their behalf. The town's officials also made proclamation to the people to *'shutt their dore, & clap their windowes downe'*. PEEPING TOM had other ideas. though, and drilled a hole in his shutters to observe the naked queen. Legend has it that he was struck blind for this act of disrespect!

Miss Viola Hamilton as Lady Godiva, June 22nd 1911

WCCA

Other sources suggest that Godiva actually represents the May Queen riding through the market in an act of innocence and impending fertility.

The Vale of the (Five) Red Horse(s)

The Vale of the Red Horse was literally set into the beautiful rural landscape at Edgehill in the Parish of Tysoe, South Warwickshire. Its first mention in recorded history dates to 1606 when map-maker JOHN SPEED alludes to the Red Horse of Tysoe. In 1607 WILLIAM CAMDEN in his publication Britannia wrote the following:

A great part of the very Vale is thereupon termed the Vale of the Red Horse, of the shape of a horse cut out in a red hill by the country people…

The colour of the horse was determined by the red clay soil that lay beneath the surface of the landscape at Sunrising Hill, where villagers 'scowed' the land to outline the horse for a reward of ale and cakes. The original horse, measuring around ninety metres in length, is thought to date back to the Anglo-Saxon period but other more conservative estimates think it may be of medieval design and was eventually lost to the rigours of farming in the first decade of the twentieth century.

With further reference to the Red Horse we can turn to poet MICHAEL DRAYTON who was born at Hartshill, Warwickshire in 1563, and to some lines from his work *Poly-Olbion*:

Scarce ended they their song, but Avon's winding stream,
By Warwick, entertains the high complexioned Leam:
And as she thence along to Stratford on doth strain,
Receiveth little Heil the next into her train:
Then taketh in the Stour, the brook, of all the rest,
Which that most goodly Vale of Red-Horse loveth best.

It is said that DRAYTON was a friend of SHAKESPEARE. Apparently the Bard of Stratford took little interest in the landscape and geography of the area but thankfully DRAYTON did! DRAYTON describes the area of the Forest of Arden as follows:

And near to these our thicks, the wild and frightful herds.
Not hearing other noise but this of chattering birds,
Feed fairly on the lands; both sorts of seasoned deer:
Here walk, the stately red, the freckled fallow there:
The bucks and lusty stages amongst the rascals strewed,
As sometimes gallant spirits amongst the multitude.

One anecdote suggests that SHAKESPEARE may have died

as a complication of a heavy night's drinking session with fellow playwright BEN JONSON and poet MICHAEL DRAYTON. In 1656 WILLIAM DUGDALE wrote in his Antiquities of Warwickshire Illustrated the following:

> *Within the precinct of the Mannour of Tishoe now belonging to the Earl of Northampton … there is cut upon the side of Edgehill the proportion of a Horse in a very large forme; which by reason of the ruddy colour of the earth is called the Red Horse, and giveth denomination to that fruitful and pleasant country thereabouts, commonly called the Vale of the Red Horse: the trenches of which ground where the shape of the said Horse is so cut out, being yearly scoured by a Freeholder in this Lordship, who holds certain lands there by that service.'*

This reference may sound poetic and designed for inclusion in a 17th-century tourism brochure, but maybe the thinking behind it was to preserve the landscape in one form or another, either physically or literally. The reference was indeed for a report to record any tradition or interest that might be destroyed by the Parliamentarian forces of Cromwell. There have been four more subsequent carvings of horses in this area, all of varying (and diminishing) sizes.

The Wroth Silver Ceremony

If you're in or around Knightlow Hill on Martinmas Eve (11th November unless the date falls on a Sunday when the ceremony is brought forward a day) and you like drinking before dawn then this is for you! The proceedings date back to before the earliest records of this ceremony made in 1170, as it was already an established annual event. Originally this silver tax was made payable to the Crown, the rights being sold to Sir Francis Leigh and subsequent heirs for £40 in 1629.

In effect the tax itself would be handed over by the locals to representatives of the Crown at the very last minute possible, 'before sun-rising'. That would be before sunrise as the new day didn't start until sunrise. There was no midnight clickover on the day then, so the tradition continues that the locals 'pay' and 'toast' His Grace the Duke of Buccleuch and Queensbury. His gathered-in revenue (which equates to 46 pence today) now goes towards the costs of travel, breakfasts and rum and milk hot toddies for those in attendance as well as advertising the event! The new day was deemed to begin when the charter could visibly be seen to be read, though after much pre-dawn rum and milk and the following libations and breakfast, this may well be a moot point these days! Tickets for the event are available locally and include a churchwarden's pipe and tobacco. These clay pipes are part of the package and a request has been made to lift the smoking ban to allow these pipes to be smoked on this day in the year at The Queen's Head public house at Bretford.

Maypole Dancing

This ceremony is common to England and the British Isles but deserves a mention here, mainly for the county's infamy in respect of this most ancient of traditions. Maypole dancing goes back to Pagan times and was traditionally performed on May Day or the Christian Festival of Pentecost. The fertility or fires of spring would be danced into the year in readiness for bumper crops and a fruitful year. The tradition consists of a highly decorated wooden pole, usually erected on a green space with long ribbons attached to the top of it that were many times longer than the pole. Each dancer would take a ribbon and would dance around to the sounds of local musicians, weaving the ribbons together in an intricate and colourful pattern. The pole was thought to continue the Norse traditions based in tree-lore where other beliefs see the pole purely as a phallic or solar manifestation.

Although it is traditionally seen as bringing people together through local events, there has been less than a coming together in some instances! In 1639 in Warwickshire there were reports of violence following neighbouring communities stealing each other's maypoles!

The Thomas Oken Feast

Thomas Oken was a man from a humble background. His birth date is speculative though he is believed to have lived during the reigns of Henry VII, Henry VIII, Edward VI, Mary I and Elizabeth I. Yet from this humble background he became the richest man in Warwick, and all from the proceeds of wool and woven products. He held a feast for a pound in money every year for the people of Warwick to show his benevolence, and in his will left that custom in perpetuity. The feast is still a part of Warwick's calendar of events today and outside The Thomas Oken Tearooms in Warwick a blue plaque reads:

Here lived Thomas Oken, a great benefactor to Warwick. He died here on the 29th July 1573.

He was certainly a man who made his mark!

View of part of the Compton Verney Estate
Shutterstock/jamesdavidphoto

Some traditional games of the region

Basket

This is the traditional game of 'follow the leader' in essence, though the sung rhyme is found in Warwickshire. A group of children decide who will be 'mother'. The rest will follow the 'mother' to market on the pretence of buying their mother a basket, but are mocking her all the way. At a given point the 'mother' will turn around to scold or to 'beat' her unruly children. If she catches one they become 'mother'.

The following rhyme is taken from Northall's English Folk Rhymes.

We'll follow our mother to the market
To buy a silver basket
When she comes home she'll break our bones
We'll follow our mother to market
We don't care whether we work or no
We'll follow our mother on tipty-toe

Giddy *(taken from Warwickshire Notes and Queries)*
A game where the person who is 'it' is blindfolded and stands in front of their friends reciting the following verse. At the end of each line the following instructions are given.

Giddy, giddy, gander,
Who stands yonder?

At this point the blindfolded person points in any direction towards their companions.

Little 'Bessy Baker'

If the name is correct they become it, or strangely, the named person does if incorrect!

Pick her up and shake her.

The one who is 'it' shakes the named person by the shoulders.

Give her a bit of bread and cheese.

Spring buds or leaves are given

And throw her over the water.

The blindfolded person swings the named person around under their arms. This is where the 'giddy' bit comes in!

Marriage

A verse for marriage follows which was recorded in Northants Notes and Queries and relates to Long Itchington, Warwickshire.

Down in the meadows where the green grass grows,

To see . . . . . . blow like a rose.

She blows, she blows, she blows so sweet.

Go out . . . . . . ; who shall she be?

. . . . . . made a pudding,

She made it so sweet,

And never stuck a knife in

Till . . . . . . came to eat.

Taste, love, taste, don't say nay,

For next Monday morning is your wedding day.

He bought her a gown and a guinea gold ring,

And a fine cocked hat to be married in.

Folk musicians at Kineton farmers market
Shutterstock/Lesley Rigg

Literary Notables

WILLIAM SHAKESPEARE was born in Stratford-upon-Avon on 26th April 1564 and grew up to become arguably the greatest poet and playwright this country has known. At eighteen he married Anne Hathaway, with whom he had three children. His works speak for themselves and are too numerous to detail here. However, he was the author of around thirty-eight plays and 154 sonnets as well some other works. He wrote much of his work in 'blank verse', poetry or dialogue that had rhythm without rhyme, as indeed here in an extract from Hamlet to give greater dramatic effect.

> *Sir, in my heart there was a kind of fighting*
> *That would not let me sleep. Methought I lay*
> *Worse than the mutines in the bilboes. Rashly—*
> *And prais'd be rashness for it—let us know*
> *Our indiscretion sometimes serves us well…*
> *(Hamlet, Act 5, Scene 2, lines 4–8)*

Michael Drayton

Born at Hartshill in 1563, DRAYTON published his first collection of faith-based poetry in 1591 and with the exception of forty copies had his next collection, The Harmony of the Church, destroyed by the Archbishop of Canterbury. He went on to write many pieces including the eighteen-book *Poly-Olbion*. He wrote plays for theatre syndicates but never really became known for this genre. However, he was a great advocate of the apostrophe – including double ones! A restless man and known to be a discontented one at that, he was rumoured to drink too hard and was indeed, a friend of the Bard!

William Shakespeare statue in Verona, Italy
Shutterstock/Istvan Csak

George Eliot

GEORGE ELIOT was born in Nuneaton. Born MARY ANN EVANS she took on a male pen name to get her work published. Women and literature were not taken too seriously in the mid-nineteenth century, even though that period spawned some of the greatest female literary giants. In 1841 MARY ANN EVANS moved to Foleshill just outside Coventry with her father Robert. Not long after arriving Mary met up with two young women, ELIZABETH PEARS and MARY SIBREE. Mary stayed at this address until her father's death in 1849 and then went on to go touring and living in Europe until settling in London to become a novelist.

It was during the Foleshill period that Mary met up with free thinkers and followers of strict Christian tracts at a time when her own faith was being seriously questioned. Meeting up with progressive thinkers such as THACKERAY, HERBERT SPENSER and EMERSON, she was greatly influenced by the works of Thomas Carlyle who, like Mary, had lost faith at an early age and to whose book Past and Present the letter below alludes. Mary went on to write some of the greatest novels of the nineteenth century including The Mill on the Floss, Middlemarch and Daniel Deronda. The following letter from Mary Ann (George Eliot) to Mary Sibree was sent from her Foleshill address on 10th May 1847 and illustrates Warwickshire language and speech patterns in use at the time.

Foleshill, Thursday
My dear Mary,
I obtained your direction from Mrs. Sibree this morning that I might express my regret to you for having failed in sending 'Past and Present'. I did really get the book on the very day I promised to do so, but the next day my amazing faculty of forgetting together with a bad headache made me quite oblivious of the whole affair. This is no excuse, but it is something to be penitent – 'Who with repentance is not satisfied is not of heaven, nor earth'. So says Shakespeare, & as I am very sure that you are composed of some of the earth's best mould, I am not afraid that you will withhold your forgiveness. I am so sorry that Mr. Sibree has missed the opportunity of having that thrilling book, while he is at leisure (I am sorry to hear) an invalid. Pray tell him that it is still at his service when he comes home.

Clifton must look lovely under these smiling skies. I hope you are drinking in all kinds of profit & pleasure, & will remember everything to tell me when we are tête à tête. You are missing nothing good except Mr. Macdonald's lectures. He gave one last evening on Self-educated men, & there is to be a second this evening on the State of society. This is no caviare however, but very simple food, and I dare say you are getting much better where you are. Farewell until you come like a rosy beam of morning to smile on me in my study. In a hurry as usual,
Thine, Mary Ann Evans

A few more notables of the many that are linked to Warwickshire:

RUPERT BROOKE, 1887–1915, World War I poet from Rugby

MATTHEW BOULTON, 1728–1809, Birmingham industrialist who developed metal pressing and gilding techniques

ROBERT CATESBY, 1572–1605, born in Lapworth, became

Last Whitley Bomber, Tachbrook Aerodrome 1944.
WCCA

famous for his adventures and infamous for planning the gunpowder plot with one Guy Fawkes!

RANDOLPH TURPIN 1929–1966 from Leamington. A West Indian boxer who became middleweight champion of the world in 1952

Airship at Dunsmore Heath 1914 -18.
WCCA

Two Firsts for Sport

Rugby

Team games are an ancient form of sporting activity and none more so than the game of rugby, which originates from a game of football and to which a man by the name of William Webb Ellis gave rise. It is said he disregarded the rules of the public schools' version of football at the time and picked up the ball and ran with it, thus inventing the game. The ball that is used in rugby is oval due to the shape of the pig's bladder that was inflated and used as a ball. This all happened in 1823 at Rugby School, hence the name given to the new sport.

Tennis

The game of 'Tenez' (translated as 'to take' or 'to play') was imported by the rich and famous from France probably as early as the thirteenth century. The nobility built indoor courts in their family mansions and developed the game of 'Royal' or 'Real' tennis. Henry VIII was a fan and built his tenez court at Hampton Court Palace. The Tudors loved the sport and developed rules for the courtly game. Ordinary people continued to play 'long' tennis outdoors until archery practice took over.

Lawn tennis became popular and took over many less-used croquet lawns. In 1859 Major Gem and a Mr Perera played this new lawn tennis game, then called pelota. In 1872 the same two gentlemen moved to Leamington (known for its spa waters) and created the Leamington Lawn Tennis Club, and the game was then pursued in the grounds of the Manor House Hotel.

Motorcycle float 1928.
WCCA

The game was then moved to the All England Croquet Club in Wimbledon, where in 1884 the first ladies' champion was Maud Watson of Berkswell, Warwickshire! Her prize was a basket of flowers made from silver and thought to be valued at twenty guneas.

Fact or Fiction, Truth or Folklore?

The Dun Cow

A story that begins in Shropshire finds a home in Warwickshire. Many years ago on Dunsmore Heath a savage beast by the name of the Dun Cow, which belonged to a giant, was said to roam the heath and terrify the locals. The story goes that the Cow had once been kept in Shropshire, where an old lady wanted to fill her pail from the beast's inexhaustible supply of milk. That she did, but when she went to fill her sieve as well the irate cow took exception and went on the rampage all the way to Warwickshire! So much so that the chivalrous knight Guy of Warwick took it upon himself to slay the beast to impress his love, 'the fair Phelice'. One of the large bones of the unfortunate beast is still in the custody of Warwick Castle, while others are said to exist elsewhere and are reported to be the horns and bones of the savage Dun Cow. They are all in fact whalebones or elephant tusks!

The Coughton Wager

In 1811 a wager (bet) was considered as to whether a coat could be made in a day for the highly influential Sir John Throckmorton of Coughton (pronounced Coton). The Throckmortons were a staunch Catholic family and had connections with Mary, Queen of Scots and Guy Fawkes, who was behind the Gunpowder Plot to destroy the Houses of Parliament in 1605.

On 25th June 1811 a hundred guineas was bet and so a sheep was sheered of its wall, the wool washed, carded, spun and dyed before being woven, cut and sewn. The whole process took thirteen hours and twenty minutes and the resulting coat is exhibited at Coughton Court, which is now in the care of the National Trust.

Stratford Fair.
WCCA

Houses in Stratford-upon-Avon
Shutterstock/Tupungato

Witches and stones

On the Oxfordshire border stands a Bronze Age stone circle known as the Rollright Stones. Many stories exist relating to this circle at Long Compton but the favoured tale of origin – which, however, is somewhat out of kilter with the dates of the stones – is as follows:

When Rollo the Dane invaded Britain he was told by a mystic or soothsayer: *'When Long Compton you shall see, King of England you will be!'*

Several battles and their victories had brought Rollo to Long Compton. As he looked over Warwickshire from this high point he descended to check out the lands that lay ahead, where he came upon the Long Compton witches who turned him and his comrades to stone. The stand-alone stone of the circle is said to be King Rollo, the nearby circle of stones is said to be his army and the four other stones set back at a distance are reputed to be the 'whispering knights' who were planning to overthrow Rollo's position. When you stand within the main stone circle it said that it is impossible to count the stones and get the correct number. Try it for yourselves!

Well, thanks for coming along on this journey throug Warwickshire, a region of rich lands and language to boot! I hope my feodary of content has got you in fair fettle to find your own way through this beautiful and ancient land. Don't forget your batch to help you enjoy a screase on the way, don't listen to the blabs and when the day is done find yourself a hostelry where the fayre is anything but scantling!

Don't be a slug-abed: get thee shoon on and go tat-tar's along the cuts, the corseys and the jittys, aside the plecks and pikes to find the real Warwickshire for theeself!

Whadya reckon?